T0013567

Hank on First!

How Hank Greenberg Became a Star On and Off the Field

by Stephen Krensky

illustrated by
Alette Straathof

For Davis, Logan, and Alex,
who will soon be playing ball, too.
—SK

To all readers who dream big.
You can do it!
—AS

Apples & Honey Press
An Imprint of Behrman House Publishers
Millburn, New Jersey 07041
www.applesandhoneypress.com

ISBN 978-1-68115-599-9

Text copyright © 2022 by Stephen Krensky
Illustrations copyright © 2022 by Behrman House Publishers

Photograph on page 32 courtesy of the National Baseball Hall of Fame
and Museum. Used with permission.

All rights reserved. No part of this publication may be translated,
reproduced, stored in a retrieval system or transmitted, in any form
or by any means, electronic, mechanical, photocopying, recording or
otherwise, for any purpose, without express written permission from
the publishers.

Library of Congress Control Number: 2022016725

Design by Elynn Cohen
Art Direction by Ann D. Koffsky
Edited by Dena Neusner
Printed in China

9 8 7 6 5 4 3 2 1

"Play Ball!"

Young Hank Greenberg was twenty-three years old, and he had the best job ever—playing first base for the Detroit Tigers. He had been there for a year now, and starting each new game was still just as exciting as it had been on his very first day.

Hank on first! It was almost too good to be true.

Almost.

Not everyone was happy to see Hank on the field.

Many people at the time saw Jews as different and treated them unfairly. The fans made fun of Hank from the stands.

"Here comes the Jew Boy."

"Throw him a pork chop. He can't hit that."

Other Jewish players had changed their last names to hide their religion. Not Hank. Being Jewish was as much a part of him as his height, his strength, or his love of baseball. He was not going to pretend to be something he wasn't.

Hank had loved baseball his whole life. Growing up, he thought about it at school, at home—and even at the dinner table.

Sports, though, didn't matter to the Greenbergs.

"Someday you will be a doctor," said his father in Yiddish, the language Jewish people spoke in Romania, where he was from.

"Or a lawyer," his mother added.
"The choice is yours."

But Hank knew what he liked. And that meant playing baseball better and better. Every day he spent hours hitting, fielding, and throwing.

When his friends wanted to stop, he shook his head. "Not yet," he insisted. Even an extra minute would help.

When no friends were around,
he paid other neighborhood kids
to run down fly balls for him.

After high school, Hank was offered a contract to play in the minor leagues. This was his big chance, but it wasn't all fun and games. The equipment was old,

the food was bad,

and the travel was tiring.

And there was something else.

One day at practice, he noticed another player staring at him.

"What are you looking at?" Hank asked.

"Just you. I heard you were Jewish."

Hank nodded. "See anything interesting?"

"I don't understand it," said the player. "You look just like anybody else."

Imagine that, thought Hank.

Hank's difficulties followed him to the majors. Even now, in the middle of a winning season, Detroit fans still heckled him for being Jewish when he came to bat or played first base.

BOOO!!!

They yelled and shouted. They booed and cursed.

Players on other teams did the same.

Hank was hurt and frustrated. Most of his teammates weren't standing up for him. They were just letting it happen.

What if he yelled back at the fans himself? Would that make him feel better? Maybe, but Hank didn't want anyone to think they were getting under his skin. So he kept quiet and let his hits and RBIs speak for him instead.

BLECH!!

The weather was hot that summer of 1934, but Hank's bat was hotter. In July and August, he had ninety hits and drove in fifty-three runs. By September, the Tigers were leading the league.

SEPTEMBER

						1
2	3	4	5	6	7	8
9 Rosh Hashana	10	11	12	13	14	15
16	17	18	19 Yom Kippur	20	21	22
23	24	25	26	27	28	29
30						

But coming up were two important Jewish holidays—Rosh Hashanah and Yom Kippur. Traditionally, most Jews didn't work on those days. And Hank's work was playing baseball.

AUGUST

					1	2	3	4
	7	8	9	10	11

For Hank, the choice was simple. He wasn't going to play.
But it wasn't that simple to the fans. They were furious.
How could Hank let them down?

"Of course I don't want to miss a game," Hank tried to
explain. "I feel bad about it."
But his religion came first.

Just to make sure, though, Hank spoke to a local rabbi for some advice. The rabbi told him that Rosh Hashanah is a celebration, which Hank understood to mean he could play.

And so Hank did just that, hitting two home runs to help win the game.

But Yom Kippur was different. On this most important holiday, all Jews prayed to be forgiven for their sins. Hank didn't need to ask a rabbi about that.

"Who cares!" said the fans. Every day they yelled at Hank—on and off the field. He was selfish and stupid, they said.

I wish the fans could see things my way, Hank thought. But that wasn't going to happen. Their minds were made up.

Then again, so was his.

When Hank woke up on Yom Kippur, he thought about staying home instead of going to a nearby temple for services. He would have no friends or family there. And if he went out, people on the street might stare or yell at him.

Still, temple was where he belonged.

When Hank arrived, the service had already begun. He didn't recognize anyone. And yet many members of the congregation clearly recognized him. They stood up, looked right at him, and started clapping.

The Tigers lost the game that afternoon. The next day the newspapers were filled with angry articles and angrier letters. It seemed like almost everyone was mad at Hank.

But there was also a poem in the newspaper. It recognized Hank's achievements—and how more people were accepting him as a Jewish ballplayer.

And it ended with a message for the fans:

HANK GREENBERG

We shall miss him on the infield and shall miss him at the bat. But he's true to his religion— and I honor him for that!

And with Hank leading the way, the Tigers kept on winning and put themselves in the World Series.

In that contest, the lead swung back and forth. It looked good when the Tigers went up three games to two. But in the end, the St. Louis Cardinals defeated them four games to three.

Tigers fans were crushed. Hank was too. But one game was not going to define his career. "Wait till next year," he told himself. He was just getting started.

Of course, not everything that mattered had happened on the field. While Hank went on to be a top player over the course of many years, staying true to his beliefs had already made him a star.

About Hank Greenberg

Henry Benjamin Greenberg was born in 1911. Also known as Hammerin' Hank or Hankus Pankus, he was the first Jewish superstar in American team sports. He faced a lot of anti-Semitism over the course of his career, but he stood by his Jewish roots and never let the attacks keep him down. Looking back over his career, he stated that while he was playing, he wanted to be "known as a great ballplayer, period." But now he wanted "to be remembered as a great Jewish ballplayer."

Hank was named the American League's Most Valuable Player in 1935 and 1940, and was a five-time All-Star before retiring in 1948. He was inducted into the Baseball Hall of Fame in 1956.

But Hank's most lasting achievement was balancing the private and public parts of his life. He stood up for what he believed in, while still playing the game he loved. At the time Hank played, there were only white faces in baseball's major leagues. And when other players faced prejudice in the future, whether about religion or race, Hank's example was there as an inspiration to them as well.